Henrik Priedola Tilly

Fleeting Meaning

Illustration: Henrik Priedola Tilly and L.P.Tilly

Förlag: BoD – Books on Demand, Stockholm, Sverige
Tryck: BoD – Books on Demand, Norderstedt, Tyskland
ISBN: 978-91-8057-572-0

Table of Contents

The Departing Drops
Atop a gilded mast blew colours of a flag
unrecognized. A graceful gesture
of the sinking ship was the fastening of its flag.
It was rushed to break and rupture
by the departing drops of a muddy hourglass
but not before or for
a passing still moment: holding its flag aloft.
And after and despite, the waters did not stir.
Amidst the set soar of the departing drops,
heaving themselves against the mast that,
broken and ruptured, set loose its sails,
the flag flew free of arrival over the still sea.

Vulnerable wonder
"Abusers come in auspicious guises
or as windswept storm survivors
or plainly with a slice to offer,
and to some, abusers come infrequently,
and some they only pass by,
but some they entangle and lead into a dance
that lasts a lifetime.
They capitulate their hearts,
whip their own backs,
curse every breath and every step,
all to understand their abuser,
for they are entangled,
and in their captivity they are made vulnerable.
"Run, run, far, far away..."
but only some may heed those words
for abusers seldom settle for a single dance-partner.
Some can leave their loved ones behind,
but some will stay and dance till death.
In the end, abusers destroy themselves,

and many will say good riddance,
but to those who've witnessed an abuser
take their loved one into that destruction,
there is no goodbye, no good riddance,
for they've died a little too,
and the world lost
their colour,
their splendour,
their vulnerable wonder."

An Obscene Gift
an obscene gift walked along a drowned shore
captured sight was free from its descent from heaven
black, dull sea stirred below, vice of a tear's soar
emblazoned on the sea: a frail reflection
of gifted skies' closing eye, beyond voice
of high strung tides, lit by afterglow's gradation
into fortress ruins alive anew by wishful choice
by its touch they wrestled once more in wills' rendition
ghosts that rose and fell over sheets of falling dust
its hand recoiled, they turned to dust in lust
having glimpsed the moving gift exempt from rest
what cannot always be but we seek it out nonetheless

A smile
if there had ever been a grimace
which could have been taken for a smile
surely it would have been one not even seen
not noticed at all
kept to oneself and never shared

The play has not ceased

the play of buds may cease of generous life's glee
but the petals' desired response is kept
a magpie with a silver ring soars in ceremony
a lone sparrow perches solemnly in the light
in dawn's first breeze past branches forming crowns
the blackbird's calls carry across a veiled construct
the crying shack, over manyfold solemn, soaring calls,
remains misplaced, and in noting its derivation, lost
as it flails with its claimant's fatigue distinct
from the relinquishing of a silver ring
atop a magpie's nest where flocks have gathered
to mark its symbol, the Sun, and of dawn to sing
as the crowning branches gave way to praise that lived
those little petals falling

Stars from a shallow cave

If out of a shallow cave by a slump
Rejected lay a knave in a heap of serving trays
Restless sprites of dawning light would still trump
In the wake of wonder at gaping night's long lost stars
And if by forfeit or conquest his self was lost
And precious, deep, empty mold used to draw
Both Crown and Plough like a beggar to a pig roast
As he was as if the last child of Man's host
Restless sprites of dawning light would still triumph
In the wake of wonder at gaping night's long lost stars.
But if he dares to measure worth in art's embrace,
Not in victories won or sorrows faced,
His words shall weave wonder, leaving a trace,
Among the stars lost in time and space.

Wholeness

Behold the grand illusion,
That consciousness weaves, a deceptive fusion.
For in truth, there lies not separate entities,
But a singular essence, the universe's symphony.
To perceive oneself as distinct, a fallacy it seems,
A misnomer, a falsehood, a mere figment of dreams.
For what are we without the Sun's radiant light,
Without the electromagnetic field, our guiding might?
And what of the plants, the biosphere's embrace,
Without their presence, what would be our space?
Though distinctions may arise, a perception of divide,
In truth, they are intertwined, forever unified.
Unintentional separation, a mistake in disguise,
Mistake theory and externalities, where confusion lies.
But intentional division, conflict theory's cruel reign,
War, oppression, and suffering, the fruits of such pain.
The root of all problems, the world's endless strife,
Lies in *NOT* perceiving from wholeness, the source of life.
To benefit oneself, at the expense of inner peace,
Internal conflict arises, a battle that won't cease.
To benefit at the cost of another, a traditional clash,
Leads to resentment, a fire that burns with a harsh flash.
And if one group prospers, while another is oppressed,
The harmony of our species, the biosphere, is suppressed.
So let us awaken to the truth of our interconnected fate,
Embrace the wholeness, the implicate order that awaits.
For in unity lies the answer, the path to harmony's door,
Where separate illusions dissolve and oneness we restore.

Fleeting Meaning

as the water and the air in the parable of the jar
so do meaning and meaninglessness align
a woman walked along a road with a jar of water
balanced on her head
there was a small crack in the jar
and as she walked the jar emptied out
when she arrived at journey's end
the jar was empty of water but full of air
as it emptied out it filled up
so too at first there was meaning
or meaninglessness and a space in between them
of struggle and conflict
the subjective desire for meaning
and the objective perspective through which
the arbitrariness of the subjective is revealed
when in fact it is through the feeling
of meaninglessness
that the desire and search for meaning is created
where meaning is subjectively attributed
there was once meaninglessness
as it is emptied out it is filled in
there can be no meaning without
meaninglessness but
if meaninglessness inevitably leads to meaning
then there can be no meaninglessness
meaninglessness is meaning
as it is emptied out it is filled in

In-between the spaces
a vestige of a sword
on uncut grass
the imprint of it's
heaviness
draw on the air
conjure and refer
what you said when you cried
you felt it so much more

Sordid disbelief
if they stand in sordid disbelief, let them
frolic with minds barer than their bodies
wander the lands, a phantasm
like a great Becoming
gliding past Being and Nothing
removing their contradictions

A mass passed across
an array of kindled eyes
a mass passed across
linked they made a thing that
had not lived before
their tracks stirred up dust and left it
behind in a single smoke cloud in their wake
searchlights of filtered want played on that cloud
those keen loops of light all bound
as lit kindling whose flickering had failed
to set back the eyes in their sockets

The Year Without a Summer

As a pebble skipping the surface of the waters
sinks absorbed by every particle, so too do bricks
crashing amidst the boiling fire. An uncaring force stirs;
a force most strange when it is silent and silent it remains.
Last it arose the sky carried a scar over rising waters.
In 1815 Mount Tambora denied that year its summer:
the largest eruption of recorded history;
cutting into the sky; absorbed by every particle.
Behemoths trembled at the waking god
as the Sun was denied its perch among her children.
The Artic waters warmed as global winds waned:
draughts, floods, famines, epidemics, chaos
with thousands dying and hundreds of thousands
becoming homeless beggars as crops and livestock died.
Switzerland laid bloody and bare
in The Year Without a Summer!
As in our system, the wealthy spared no expense
and left no food for purchase for the victims.
Perpetual rains confined the wealthy indoors
as the rest searched for illusory wild roots.
No such storms had been beheld
and amidst the blackness: our turned, blind eye.
Amongst the wealthy, was Mary Shelley,
whose Creature character could easily be seen
as a memory of the victims she saw:
extraordinarily deformed and diseased,
shunned and disregarded by society!
Perhaps in the cruel Creature
they are demonized, as they were
by the local newspapers with antagonistic rhetoric,
or perhaps she recognized in them
the waking god's power
and human fragility's beauty!
What if they had done as the Creature?

Conformity

conformity, conformity
those perceived to be at the very centre
of that cultural normalcy worry
whether they do in actuality conform,
while unknowingly appear to others
as perfectly inhabiting
an ideological ideal when really
any will do if the goal is to feel superiority
the darker achievement of conformity
is our separation into Us and Them

The rivers of commons

its self-propagation is ubiquitous in the binary world
a secondary evolution of our rented Earth
to separate it from us
the sediment a river has moved long ago
and moves still in their intimate relation
from the closed sanctuary of the High Faith
pillars arraigned of perfectly white pebbles
a reorientation of access to the sacred
a flooding of that arid, private land
Reformation; translation; dissemination
private pebbles were released and carried
from ancient hand to plurality of tongues
a river that does not dry presses forward
likewise the sacred earthworks of Hopewell
the pre-Columbian Americans raised
with the mud of their rivers
literal capturing of the sacred
gods and lives written in spatial form
each passing layer moving away
reforming; reshaping the private into the river
where nothing is private, kept away

the purpose of the private is to be shared
a river that does not dry will press forward
the secondary evolution continues
not before long all private pebbles
the rivers of commons shall carry away

A Moment's Ending

Permeating the air, a hum, steady and dreary
carrying no incentive, only confident serenity.
A steady hum ushered the ball of blue, brown,
and white wonder
into cold and cathartic oblivion.

The hum reached a dimly lit oil drum,
its lit fire flickered and barely remained lifesome.
There, under the roof of a tiny, disused shelter
stood a sentient shape in solemnity of silent soulfulness
and in salient sapience, grave gravity, of its moment's ending.
Indignant of drumming downpour, thunderous uproar rending
the ageless shelter, in sleepless night, into silly windswept swaying.
Till the crackling of its clothes, with Capricorn character, burning
with flame's fervorous finality carried its mind into memory maze.
The lavishing, luminous lovers undulated, illuminating
a face of faraway gaze
belonging to one who, akin to ancient ancestor,
cardinal company kept: fire and thunder
but in final moment's end thought of love's heartful pleasure.

Caught in memory maze, at behest
of intermingling of crackling and drumming.
Bare to irresistible memory, turned to bear
intermingling of past passion and present pain.

Above it all, a divine decree of Enki the wise, the primordial Capricorn:

"Soulful heart, Heartful soul!
One is incapable of possessing the other.
Yet if they are never known and near to one another,
they shall know silence eruptible
and only hungry intimacy.
But the threat of afflictive fate is not irresoluble
for they are drawn to one another. Irresistible
is the amorous attraction
of the two that complete each other."

with Enki's sage words
it thought of her
smiling openly with her eyes
giggling and filled with butterflies
adoring her lively presence
her graceful gestures
her lips, how they had moved
the warm peace they had shared
the fantastic feeling of
freedom from thoughts forlorn
her torrid tone when she had been tenderly,
reaching out and touching softly
and that it had loved her for love's sake
as it listened to the crackling and the drumming

A steady hum ushered the ball of blue, brown, and white wonder
into cold and cathartic oblivion,
no more drums
no more shelter
no more primordial deity
Capricorn or other.
At its final moment's ending,
it thought of her heartful soul's and its soulful heart's
intermingling pleasure.

My fate is cast

Oh, wretched pleas, no hope to be found,
My fears doth grow tightly bound.
For when I beseech Fortune's aid,
Her ears doth close, my cries doth fade.
With beeswax from Ulysses' past,
Her deafness reigns, my fate is cast.

Innocence

"The loss of innocence...
it follows you wherever you go.
In the light as in the dark, you are a changed thing.
And there is now one, for you alone to know,
that you will never be."
"What would we be without it?"
"I dare not ponder.
Still frolicking in the garden, I assume.
Though it may be blasphemous for some,
I doubt you would object,
if I gave a blessing towards that prevalent serpent."

The unsaid

As what is said can divide us
so, the unsaid can be a divide preventing us from coming together at all.
Pre-conceived notions, expectations, assumptions, inferences:
all when left unsaid can only function to divide.

Whispers carried by the wind,
Words spoken can create a rift within.
But in the realm of silence, unseen,
Lies a divide that keeps us apart, it seems.
Unspoken thoughts, a chasm deep,
A barrier that hinders unity's keep.

For preconceived notions and hidden desires,
Can only serve to fuel division's fires.
In the realm of the unspoken,
Lies the power to keep us broken.
For assumptions and expectations untold,
Can build walls the meek cannot unfold.
The unspoken words, a silent divide,
Keeping us apart, unable to coincide.
For inferences and judgments left unsaid,
Can only lead to separation widespread.
As what is voiced can tear us apart,
The unspoken can shatter unity's heart.
For preconceived notions and hidden beliefs,
Can only sow discord:
like bleeding autumn's, falling leaves
and bloodied, golden, falling apples.

The Bond
denial in the face of
what is to be faced
down to the bone the bond
the inexorable congruence

Recognition
"Not only those absent from our side,
Even those opposed, they too abide,
For one cannot sever from the current of time's tide",
They jested with joy and relief; battle's tension defied.

The Münchhausen trilemma

Regarding knowledge, the Münchhausen trilemma slyly dances,
A thought experiment, revealing truth's elusive chances.
It aims to show the impossibility, theoretical and grand,
Of proving any truth, even in logic's sacred land.
For when we seek to know, and find certainty's embrace,
We find ourselves entangled in a perplexing maze.
If asked how a proposition is known to be true,
Proof may be presented, a glimmer of hope anew.
But alas, the question persists, like an echoing refrain,
What of the proof itself, can it too be explained?
And so the trilemma unfolds, with its threefold plight,
A closed room with no escape, no respite in sight.
First, the circular argument, a loop that never ends,
Where the proof relies on the proposition it defends.
A dizzying dance of self-reference, a paradoxical display,
Worse than simply trapped in a cycle, forever to stay.
Then comes the regressive argument, a never-ending quest,
Each proof demanding another, an infinite behest.
A labyrinth of proofs, stretching into the abyss,
With no final destination, no ultimate bliss.
Lastly, the dogmatic argument, a stance of blind belief,
Resting on accepted precepts, without any relief.
Asserted rather than defended, it stands on shaky ground,
Leaving reason behind, in favour of faith profound.
Thus, the Münchhausen trilemma reveals its profound decree,
That in the realm of knowledge, truth remains a mystery.
No matter the path we choose, no matter how we strive,
Proving any truth seems impossible, yet we seem to thrive?

Luxury
a coastal town seen from a hill
a high vantage point creating picturesque beauty
that need not be present
unavailability in separation, in distance
in imagining what lives in each detail
without ever being present
in the joy or the tragedy
breezy remoteness in all its reserved luxury

Tragedy of the Commons
In a village green, where farmers roam,
Their livestock graze, free to roam.
Each seeks to gain, to profit more,
Adding more beasts, to the field they adore.
But as they do, the pasture fades,
Overgrazed and worn, unable to sustain.
Their collective interest, now betrayed,
By personal gain, they cannot maintain.
The multipolar trap, a force so strong,
Drives them to exploit, the shared resource long.
Their actions lead, to degradation and harm,
A tragedy of the commons, a collective alarm.

None freer
There are none freer than they who refuse
To bow their wills to any force or might,
Except when they choose to be subdued,
And willingly submit to power's right.

The Prisoner's dilemma

In game theory, a tale unfolds,
Where two souls face a choice, their destinies unfurl.
The Prisoner's dilemma, a concept profound,
Cooperation or betrayal, their paths are bound.
Should both choose to cooperate, a reward awaits,
A moderate payoff, a shared fate.
Yet, if one should betray, while the other remains true,
The betrayer reaps high, the cooperator, a low accrue.
But should both choose betrayal, a sombre scene,
A negative payoff, a bitter routine.
This dilemma, a web of deceit and despair,
Where choices intertwine, leaving hearts laid bare.
A multipolar trap, this dilemma reveals,
A conflict ensnares, as darkness conceals.
For multiple souls, entangled in strife,
Suboptimal outcomes, the price of their life.
Though cooperation beckons, a path to unite,
The allure of betrayal casts fuel and ignites.
Thus, both players suffer, their fortunes decline,
A multipolar trap, where escape is confined.
In this intricate dance, where choices collide,
The Prisoner's dilemma, a truth we can't hide.
For it mirrors a world, where actors entwined,
Face consequences, their destinies defined.

Faltering step

Under what suns in what shadows
do we step
of whom we carry with us
in each fallen step
their tearing faces, their lonely hearts
wanted my deft touch
the strength I had to spare

its sudden absence predicated no applause at all
the curtain did not fall
left on stage with no script
they dance their half reciting the absence of their suns
the presence of their shadows
I leave myself
let a mime lasso me
be the hook, the hand that threw and the prey
sing the chorus line
fill the vacant lot at the kick line
play pretend with the kick-off referee and no team
them and me; my next sun and I
it will be different no more shadows
climb the stage
I will be present, do you believe that?

Connecting

As I endeavour to connect with you and Wholeness
my lips quiver and my voice falters.
The songs of my soul both grim and graceful
with feeling and memory in my consciousness lulled
reverberate ungracefully in every embodied nerve.
Its disharmonies soar and delve
reconnecting from the obscure boundary of my earthly drive.
In exclaiming the songs of my soul lies a persistent occupation,
defied by an ignorant body and an occupied people,
teared at the barbed gates of my own critical perception,
to reach sublimity and wholeness in a body made supple and regal,
whence my voice would no longer be feeble.

The Gatekeeper

"Power, Control...
power, control..."
What is success to a gatekeeper?
To a gatekeeper
what is the soul in man's work?
Sand out of glass;
ink out of letters;
clay out of tablets...
A gatekeeper will sort
every grain of sand
and call it work.

no glass; no letters; no tablets
empty plains
a lone voice atop a hill
of criticized sand whispering:
"Power...Control...Power...Control..."

Inner child's prejudice

The scabbard, cast into the briny deep,
The handle lost, the naked blade's parts weep,
Once used to push aside the Fates' decree,
Now set aside, its innocence set free.
A tool of agency, brought forth by will,
Now lies in ruin, its purpose unfulfilled.
A sense of injustice, etched upon its grip,
With no more pity left to beg.
But what if it's not the case,
That one must give chase,
To the inner child's prejudice?

Shadow

gripping
feeling
enveloping
a shadow rises when you fall
takes your place
you become the past
a cold heart
that yearns for warmth
you are left with knees on the ground
unmoving
open palms
facing the sky
falling
your shadow glances back
but leaves you
draining
piping
missing

A Cynic Supreme

a great disillusionment
forcing reality out of
imagined orders
peer leaders do battle
sacrifice lesser pawns
to frothing aggression
he is a lesser pawn
he is a young cynic

an institution calls out
born of beliefs of what man is due
the cynic wants to belong; the cynic ascends the ranks
of both wisdom and learning

time heals all wounds
but how much do we learn?
the cynic is reborn of sweat and tears
he takes a place amongst the walls of the institution
sees the world through their glass doors
there is a reason people believe
in an order; imagine
they can have it all
but in reality; imagine
it is all imagined
he is betrayed
his elders who are the institution
who have the power
do with it what they will not what they should
the promise is defeated
a race without a finish line
no tape to run through
the tape recording their speeches has worn out
dust in the cynic's eyes
the race is extended
he must run on
through fog and night
through hail and sleet
through sand and flame
they will it so
in an imagined order a believer runs and runs
runs themselves silly
but the man was reborn through sweat and tears
now he is a cynic supreme

Sleight of structure

more of it
  but easier to solve
less of it
  but sticky
 and ingrained
  into the matter
where it resides

Sweet Pain

Culled from Light's ambition
Shaped in wilful sedition,
of Light's goodwilled vision,
in faulty forerunner tradition,
into King with antler crown
with potential
to bring about a dark star rising.

An overbearing phantom in search
of sacrificial lamb, Light's patron, floating
slightly and silently above darkening earth.
His flesh was ash from damned, crying
soul's cold hearth
his crimson robe was billion moving mites
clung to him with jabbing jaws, jamming wide berth
of, held and erected, fearful Light's moral heights.

Swarms of monarch butterflies bursting
from depths unheard of was royal, priming precursor
to sweet, sustained pain's severe harbinger,
whose pale moonlight spotlight shines
on none other than you.
And as your eyes multiply by memory motor
to encompass all those you gave your heart to possess

on a stage built for you, you'll feel all eyes
on you.

His promise: release you into the bare and boundless
after sweet, sustained pain's end leaves you careless
like a fruit fly drowned in mead.

When is it love?
what is not perverted
is my flesh not a tool for your pleasure
a body as a fetishistic object
when is the real alone with itself
it is not encumbered with fantasy
the real is one with fantasy
we are not props in each other's interaction only
when we love or that is when we value it above reproach
beyond cynicism

The Same Coin
when did we censor, when did we torture
horrid violence practised by the state
and politically-correcting our language
to protect from symbolic violence
became commonplace
at the same time
a coin that falls on both sides
a gavel made of paper
a pen filled with blood

Freedoms of ancient Americans
how did they live; how could you know
those forebears defining distant
with freedom to abandon one's community
be welcomed far-away
with freedom to shift back and forth
between social structures with the seasons
with freedom to disobey authority
if authority over-reached
how could they live; how do you know
we have to be as rigid as we are?

Kindness
Kindness, a bonfire, radiant and bright
We yearn to bask in its comforting light,
Rest peacefully among its familiar crackling,
Yet, someone must gather the firewood, light the way,
To be the first to show kindness, come what may.
Not all strive to be vulnerable enough to take that chance
But you have felt its embrace, a step or two in life's dance.
Take solace in knowing that you have felt its warmth,
And make it your duty to light the next fire.
It only burns if you let it,
Otherwise, 'tis the difference between surviving and living.

On the end of that day
Drifting, drifting...
The murky waters settled.
The ferryman rowed ever onward for the next, for the next.
Drifting into soft tender darkness... My sense of self lost.
A nude babe running, shrieking with shaking fists.
There was something to know now for something had been lost,
and much more had been seen and heard.
With each cold chill of night, with each passing wind,
bringing warmth of new days, more of the old was swept away,
and more of the new was uncovered raw and exposed.
I knew then who I was not and that provided unimaginable comfort,
and I wept tears of unknowable feeling that felt to be mine
and mine alone,
on the end of that day.

Power
"Power, power!"
What quality should I assign to you
so I may safely think you are not for me?
Should your truth be hidden?
Your conformity and non-radicality sheathed
beneath a mask of coarse outbursts and
stimulating provocations.
"I burn, I burn!", I beg of you!
Allow me to ignore your ordinariness!
Should you change definitions?
Assertions on the natural world,
assertions on the private world,
going round and round, circularly:
that is not this and this is not that
no, no, not that but *that*; not this but *them*.
Now I am burned, and you are alone,
"Power, power! Where have you gone?"

Impersonal equivalence
to it you appear as a constant sleeper
it prays you never wake
while all your deepest desires revolve
around what it cannot give

Your exquisite, unparalleled allure and rich past
Goes unnoticed, disregarded, fading fast
The vibrant hues you envision in your dreams
Are but blades, numbers in disguise, it seems
Equity claims to offer fairness, this pallid language it speaks
Justifying its actions, the ends it seeks
Yet in its pursuit, it ensures without fail
That beautiful souls fall short, their dreams derailed
These beautiful souls, mere pawns indentured in its game
Labouring, enslaved, their lives never the same
Destined to live and perish in such a plight
Their beauty overshadowed, hidden from sight

Promises, once personal, now Cold and Detached
Bureaucracy, the embodiment of Sovereignty, power Unmatched
In a world where Our Lives are reduced to Mere Sums
Disparities Arise, Legal Equalities Succumb

Strings of yellow eyes
Through the ebony shroud of night, echoes of anguish resound,
Strings of yellow eyes, a chorus of scratchy howls profound,
Distinct as raindrops or blueberry leaves, they seem,
Yet, united they made the night their witness, a personal maelstrom,
Enveloping my non-yellow eyes.

The Tale of August

There was once a man
broad and strong with long running hair
with a smile did he say, "I can!".
Ploughed the lands he did with care
and August was his name.
Until one day a great wolf came,
and challenged the man to a dare.
Smiling as ever he agreed to the game,
which was to travel far and wide
bringing back three things rare.
To Wican's forests he went in search of hide
of the loveliest and fastest hare.
Nor man nor woman of any height
had ever caught a speedster this fair.
He tried and tried and even for naught
was his great thundering might.
Heaving and heaving he was left in the dust,
but give up his smile he would not without a fight,
and in his will and smile he did not lose trust.
He ran all day and all night
until he became part of the wind,
and forever such wind be called gust.
Now he had the hare he sought.
Off he ran to Riverrose for the next rarity to find.
From a great and terrifying beast
he desired it's teeth.
Stealthy it was and proud of mind
dragging prey unaware to sunken depth.
Such a sight left him lame;
in its eyes he saw cold death.
For prey were lucky if it did them only maim...
For a full day and night he did naught but quiver,
but nor his smile nor his will did he let melt.
When opening its jaw it was weak, he saw from cover.

Stealth he learned from it, waiting to spring like a bolt.
Afraid he was that it would him sever,
but not of being called a dolt,
as he tied around its jaw his belt.
Heading back to Timbermere
feel he did mightily worn,
though overcome he had his fear,
and there was no loss to mourn.
Then from over a hill, he did hear
a song from a most beautiful voice.
An urge overcame him, see the source he must.
Blind he was to any other choice.
Clambering up the hill, he felt his words rust.
Atop the hill he tripped, cursing nature's vice.
After falling down the hill he landed in a heath,
and from anger he began to seethe.
Cut, scraped with pants loose he was a mess,
looking as if his mind was devoid of breadth,
but when he saw her it seemed not all was amiss,
although he felt like the pest.
She took his breath with her dress.
He could not suspend his zest:
he spoke of himself and of his fall, but he did miss
that she lacked all sight.
He wished then that he did speak less,
and felt worse after making a jest,
but she laughed and laughed, he had suffered no loss.
He spoke of her song and did so dearly,
and of his journey as well with every detail nearly.
She felt his face and smile and liked him clearly.
She agreed to come along,
but she said if he did her wrong
he would hear a different song.
Finally he had come home
to his simple abode.

Thought he did of all the land he had to roam.
His rarities were light, but had become a heavy load,
as the wolf came close spewing foam.
He spoke for long about the road,
as if reciting a tome;
he feared the future of his treasure.
The wolf asked to see what was up for measure,
and looked upon the maiden speaking pleasure.
August said to look but not touch.
The wolf did not heed him much.
He pounced on the maiden with force such,
it sent her into a rage.
She sang with sound of mage,
and the song brought forth, and threw him in, a cage.
August looked around and saw no other rarity.
He asked the wolf for clarity.
The wolf confessed, showing his quality.
The maiden spoke to August of his avidity
claiming it was a liability.
He could not resist to revere her ability
and spoke of her passionately.
She reached out to his face, and felt his smile
love and honesty she felt but no guile.
His lacking did her no more rile
for he had won her over with his smile.

erasure
The erasure of what could be,
A void where possibilities flee,
In this vast expanse of nothingness,
Where everything is lost no less.
The wind, once sharp, now dulled,
As the spring's arrival is lulled,
A sinking feeling, heavy and deep,

Thunder and crashing, no longer steep.
For they cannot touch this earthly ground,
Their purpose and meaning, no longer found,
In contemplating this eternal plight,
We pass through time, day and night.
But when we recite, only tears remain,
Falling softly, like a gentle rain,
And as they descend, where will they go?
To what depths will their sorrow flow?

Song From Pre-History

Through the year and through it all
Through fear and falling heads
Hearts filling with gall
And our graves, our earthy beds
To our children we send this call
Through the year and through it all
Play our flute till honey wind fills the air
Play in the sea, forget about the pall
Find your love, Oh! to be in a pair
Through the year and through it all
Hunt the buffalo, sing its praise
Beware the hidden cheetah, look for its gaze
Through the year and through it all
Remember who we used to be
Don't you let our ways fall
Look upon the Great Sea
At night above it, in those stars we beat
Your hearts to live on, to live on
Through the year and through it all

The Wheat Snake

what water is to life
wheat is to global capitalism
beginning its life as a weed among the fringe
it survived through its applicability
a balanced life was built on straw
grain was the apple of the garden
wheat has since shed its skin
and slithered into every stomach
local customs, religions be what they may
the garden is long gone
but for global capitalism
the West still stands but it may fall
it will still slither on
the state of global capitalism renders
Western cultural values as unnecessary
that snake is well and fat
even in authoritarian alternative modernity
equality, freedom, and care for all,
may be rejected or better yet reimagined to forestall
the insatiable appetite of this creature,
and preserve a future that's brighter and richer

Modern religion

In the depths of my being, a sensation resides,
A feeling I struggle to express, inadequate in words,
But as I delve into self-empathy's embrace,
I realize it's not my personal inadequacy that lingers,
Rather, an impersonal inadequacy takes its form,
And now I know the name of this formidable Beast.
To this Beast, all other faiths are but relics,
For it appeases the same fears, torments, and strife,
That ancient religions once claimed to alleviate.
An occultic creed, spreading not through texts,

But solely through certain rituals and practices.
A relentless cult devoid of mercy's grace,
Where every day is a grand celebration,
And each day commands unwavering devotion,
From every devoted follower, without respite.
No act of worship is ever deemed sufficient,
For it demands absolute commitment to its ways.
Its practices must be pursued relentlessly,
Like the Sun gods of Aztec lore, craving sacrifice.
This cult demands our very souls, it seems,
For we are compelled to partake,
As potential or real offerings upon its altar.
While old religions sought to absolve guilt,
Through atonement and forgiveness for their faithful,
This cult deliberately creates guilt,
Claiming our lives fall short due to insufficient dedication.
A guilt that finds no solace, encroaching universally,
Unprecedented, a religion of utter annihilation.
Transcendence of God may have reached its end,
But they are not deceased, rather intertwined with humanity.
Their aim is to assimilate all into an eternal, sacrificial rite,
Declaring indulgence in their practices as the remedy for all woes.
Their practice, unbridled and unregulated capitalism,
Like a potent steroid injected into mankind's veins,
We grow larger, yet increasingly frail and ailing.

Neither nor
The wounded soul who dares to voice their pains
shall guide a life of sorrow, where tragedy resides.
Yet the wounded soul who shies from strife's embrace
shall wander through life, devoid of passion's grace.

Western arrogance

The Enlightenment, a time of great thought,
Would lose its essence if freedom, equality,
Rationality, and religion were not sought,
Discussed, and debated with great clarity.
Similarly, without exchange of ideas,
Between Europeans and Indigenous Americans,
The Enlightenment would lack substance, it appears,
And be devoid of important discussions.
Modern historians reject this notion,
As they see it as western arrogance,
A projection of beliefs onto Indigenous Americans,
Romanticizing them as noble savages, a grievous offense.
But in truth, Europeans did converse,
With Indigenous Americans, coexisting,
While also contributing to their demise, perverse,
Their impact on history, significant and persisting.
Those who embraced Indigenous American ideas,
Of personal freedom and equality,
Found profound meaning in these concepts, clear,
And their contributions should not be belittled.
To dismiss the possibility of such interactions,
Is to disregard the impact of Indigenous Americans,
And ultimately reflects Western arrogance,
A failure to acknowledge their contributions, a great transgression.
Such modern historians live mired in their ideology,
So far so that they do not recognize
That their own behaviour
Is the behaviour they are condemning.

Irrevocable
And his skin fell upon his tool,
and he separated them,
without thought
without concern
for where they lay.

Summer's light
I looked toward the pink hue that so rarely bears itself
upon that liveliest of stages.
When it lies in cover it resembles the abnegation of our hope,
but in full display of lively pink it is that charming light,
that blends with itself in ever so slight waves
evolving into the orange crown jewel,
like a bud blossoming to a flower,
till wisps of light remain,
when dilapidated remnants of colour hope we accompanied its beauty.

The Darkness
escape looms over others
for whom the night's dark still calls
stars sparkle still more
hidden depths in murky waters
snakebites when far from shore

By it I know
Your pain brings me
sweet pain
it is by it I know
I yet live and am not
an uncaring beast.

What to bear

to bear a stranger
I am still surprised
to dare my heart to open
variety of human
just one
not two or even ten
I am still surprised
at the strangeness of strangers
just one with a keen openness
open heartedness
for which I am a salve
a soothing balm
a key to a lock
no more an undeniable lack
of fitting union
Begone strange strangers!
no more of my failure's reunion
but if that is the extent of our encounter
let us prolong the illusion
allow it to linger a little while longer

Three Little Mice

"Slowly they sunk, lost to us forever.
Their little mouths closed
their little whiskers, their grey-brown fur,
and their eyes black and open."
"Will no one see them and bury them?"
"There is one. One who will see them.
One who will bury them."
"Drowned in a dug ditch on abandoned land,
overgrown and unkempt.
The vegetation planted has been let run wild,
and the ever encroaching weeds of the neighbour

have not been held at bay. Slowly,
these three siblings found
their way there, unafraid
since man's scent was lost on the wind.
Before they could settle it,
and bring all their family there,
they adventured too far.
Unable to escape the deeply and steeply dug ditch, they drowned
in the collected rainwater.
To some they look at peace, to some lost, and to others
they are now made hollow."
"Will no one show reverence and honour life?"
"There is one."
"To drown in silence, to never be seen,
yet be made of the black sea of shimmering light."
"Will they not return?"
"There is one who shall meet them.
One made of ash and dust who shall dance
in the black sea of shimmering light."
"Oh, what a heart that in dirty golden autumn
black and white magpies fight
in the drained sunlight.
The jays and robins have turned to the dawning south,
the earth hardened to summer's final heat,
the worms and magots burrowed deeper,
yet on that day three mice siblings drowned
in search of a new home, and the magpies
will not stop fighting now."
"Oh, what a heart
that now lies
beneath! Oh, do see them
race to dear death departed.
Oh, but hear them
cry out to the eyes
of the black sea lights!

Oh, but there is only one ending, and in their's
silent and unseen there end we all."
"Will now not the Sun set final, set one, set all?
Will we not end with them?"
"There is one.
One through whose eyes they would be seen,
and heard, and buried, and honoured."
"To be that one, venerable throughout,
brimming with light, glowing outwards.
One to care, one to bury..."
"Will we not be lost then to us forever?"
"There is one. One who will look
upon these drowned mice
and perceive us and them all in those same eyes,
of the black sea of shimmering light.
One who in burying them will bury us.
One for whom the magpies dance.
One for whom the damned smile.
One who will sin before they love,
and struggle more than they succeed.
But they will venerate life,
and made of ash and dust, they will carry us
from sunset to sunset."
"Will we not suffer needlessly if,
our hopes are misplaced?"
"Then we would know these mice,
then we would know all who dance these seas."

It Spilled Out
It spilled out.
It overflowed, a constant debate,
Twisting and turning, never straight,
A tangled mess, a scribbled fate,
Forget the calm, the steady state.

Notice, notice!
What its hands encompass,
What its eyes behold,
Rapturing what has come to pass,
Capturing what it could not unfold,
It spilled out.
And in the midst of chaos, it found its abode,
That place, at last, sacred, and bold,
Listen to the whispers, the sparks that ignite,
Thrown and lost in the dark of night.
A boundless chase,
Pouring for sweet life's grace,
Hands in soil, keeping the land,
Love's labour, a resting hand,
Into the brightness it seeks to expand,
Into the light blessed by a venerated band,
Of three little mice seeking out new land.
It spilled out into all I had.

Self-reflection

From whence didst thy self-reflection spring?
Thou didst not choose to be endowed
With such emotional intelligence, a thing
That doth thy motives and behaviours shroud.
What fount didst thou drink from, pray tell?
To gain such insight and introspection,
That thou mayst examine thyself so well,
And ponder on thy own imperfection.
Perhaps 'twas from thy life's experience,
Or from the wisdom of those before,
That thou hast gained such competence,
To delve within and seek thy core.
Whate'er the source, 'tis a gift divine,
To know oneself and grow in kind.

In cyclical time willed against
Willed against the everlasting foamed tides
against the climbing precipices
of indignant Fate's peaks
where shrubbed rolling valleys
gather Old Gods' lustre
in mountaintop pools of pale moonlight
there none is master

Willed against the everlasting swirling tides
against the ever reaching flatlands
of emptied, hallowed Faiths
where hungry howls fill the nights
Old Gods spring from young babes
on forgotten dried blood's cracked earth
there none find their hearth

Willed against the everlasting tides
there is one who will be master
one who will find their hearth
Not just another drop in the tides

Nebulous
nebulous
moved as if by wind to dust and leaves
to have heard with the wrong kind of tongue
to have felt so much
where did it go
day by day by forces such
every soul met high and low
shrunk to ever-shrinking frame
to have known them all
now they are the same
some caught me in my fall

their faces gone with barely a name
for mine would they hit upon a wall?
to have spoken with the wrong kind of ears
the floating stage's handcrafted raft
nebulous
moved as if by wind
to dust and leaves

Falling flat
tell me, what do you want to hear
as if lost at stormy sea
blurry! what is coming near
out of the corner of my mind
speaks a counsellor
considered words
considered actions
what is to believe
adapting melodies
ill-begotten reveries
empty notes
falling flat

It is that untamed
not where is aimed
it is that untamed
heart's desire, tainted
let it come unwelcomed
Feel it. Bad and ugly, smeared
and maimed, silenced,
and unheard, let it be heard
Feel it drop and drip
out of you, let it rip
the preconceived to shreds

it knows your truths
the ones you've sheathed
under Pain's birthed
layers of rock and iced
lakes of kept and ignored tears
allow the currents of tragedy's reverence
to raise a sun and melt them away
they will pour out of you
and in time
small stems and moss
will cover layers of rocks
warm peace
might just take
its place
in you

A voice for me calls

a voice for me calls
out amongst the old world
where living is in truth
and all is

a choir behind it rises
in disregard
coalescing days and nights
we are known in our uses
and cohabiting spirits,
guests of rising glances
eyes still sparkling

it is in that wonder
their bodies quiver
two birches swaying
in the same zephyr

unbidden acts ending severely
travelling
expressing
dying
one swift moving
of the body
of the choir

Not rattling the cage
not rattling the cage
not biting, not thrusting the bars
hold on
as it flips over
and fills with water
take in a mouthful
and hold your head
above water
it'll fill with air again, and you'll be
the intruder

don't kick the waves
as they run near
to kick away the sea
fill a bucket and dig a hole
in the sand and pour it in
sit and watch in stillness
watch it be absorbed
take the mud and make something or just sit
seawater will be gone

move alongside
turn it up and around, under and over
don't just wrestle and scream
it'll consume you

I've seen it
please adapt
constant motion all your days
learn how to react

The drink of a mind adrift

Oh, what is it that makes him sniff and peer,
At something rotten, with a bitter sneer?
Once made with lemons, sugar, and boiling water,
Now it's foul, yet he drinks it still, the rotter.
Does he long for what once was, a memory sweet,
Or has he lost his taste for life's lovely treat?
What is this drink that he consumes with such thirst,
A warning of decay, yet he drinks it first?

Please exit in an orderly fashion

Amidst the woods, a tale is told
Of squirrels and nuts, a story old
When trees bear more than squirrels can eat
Some nuts escape, a lucky feat
But when the larders are packed with nuts
The mothers grow, plump and robust
Hawks and foxes, they too thrive
Their dens full; blood flows with woods alive
Yet in the next fall, the trees shut off
"Nuts are scarce", the squirrels scoff
They venture out, exposing themselves
To predators, hunger, and deadly spells
Starvation and predation take their toll
The squirrel population takes a fall
The woods grow quiet, the silence loud
But out come pecan flowers, a promise proud
And so, dear friends, please exit with care

In an orderly fashion, beware
For the woods are home to many a creature
Let's leave it as we found it, a pristine feature

The Ox and the Plough

Oh, how the buffalo roamed free,
A spirit to pray to, a life to see.
As a hunter, I can take what I need,
And use it all well, with respect indeed.
I cry when I kill, for I know its worth,
And say, "I'll be buried, part of the earth.
Grass for your great-grandchildren to eat,
A cycle of life, so complete."
But if I yoke a buffalo, make it an ox,
Cut off its testicles, bind its horns,
I cannot be animistic, cannot respect its spirit,
For tis now a dumb ox, man's dominion to inherit.
Yet, the plough, so advantageous,
Is obligate, for us to flourish,
For if we don't, we'll surely perish,
And our tribe in famine will languish.
But this technology codes,
A pattern of behaviour, that erodes,
The values of animism, so pure,
And replaces it with a culture, unsure.
Animism died with the ox-driven plough,
For beating an animal all day, we cannot allow.
So let the buffalo roam free, a spirit to pray,
And be a hunter, with respect, every single day.

In ancient times, when women gathered and men hunted,
Or when women tended gardens and men hunted,
Women still provided half the food, it's true,
But ploughing was left to men, for women might miscarry, too.

Men's strength was needed for this task,
And so they provided the majority, a mighty ask.
Women moved into the home with a new role to play,
And with it came a shift in the gods we pray.
Patriarchy arose from this change,
As ploughing gave men Power, a new range.
Food surplus was created, and with it came private property,
And sharing systems gave way to wealth inequality.
Marriage became institutionalized on a larger scale,
As men sought paternity certainty, without fail.
This led to views on animals, patriarchy, and class,
All from a piece of technology, the plough, alas.
Each piece of tech encodes game theoretic power,
Those who use it will thrive, those who don't will cower.
Just as the printing press birthed revolution and democracy,
Each piece of tech, a game of power and destiny.
For those who embraced it, a path to success,
For those who resisted, history would suppress,
The plough, a symbol of strength and progress,
Encoded in its use, a game of power, no less.

Behold, the plough, a binding force,
It shapes our conduct, sets the course.
For within its code, lies behaviour's creed,
Unveiling values, shaping minds indeed.
As it scales, its power expands,
Moulding cultures with its skilled hands.
Not solely reliant on faith's embrace,
Technology crafts our values, leaving no trace.
Hence, we must design with utmost care,
Tech that considers the values we bear.
Beyond physical costs, we must delve,
Into the human psyche, where cultures dwell.
This is axiological design, a noble quest,
Infusing ethics into tech's behest.

For infrastructure drives the superstructure,
And moulds the social fabric, ensuring its rupture.
The obligation to grow, to progress,
Compels us to embrace tech's finesse.
Yet, in this pursuit, we must beware,
Of the nihilistic superstructures that ensnare.
For intertwined are these intricate loops,
Binding us to the superorganism's troops.
Economic growth, social structure entwined,
A dance of forces, in harmony or confined.

Unclear

Falling down, a cascade of dust so frail,
In the distant light, unclear and blurred,
My vision remains unclear and pale
Thoughts neurotic, minds emboldened, collide,
Frail dust falling, planets revolving, unheard.

Thoughts neurotic, minds emboldened and strong,
Frail dust falls, as planets revolve along.

Black holes devour, consuming all in sight,
Production dissipates under blurred might.
No offsetting, no balance to be found,
The mind's creation, forever unbound
In unclear sight, beauty is bold.

Washed away

When hope's light fades away,
The unknown looms ahead,
A thousand coins flipped in play,
Lost in the tide of strange water's dread.

The Choice

To ask not what one would be without that which we
gnaw at ourselves with
rather untoward for the non-believer
a masochistic eye

night and day
black tar and the Sun's ray
rather or
neither nor
light is always waning
or growing
absolute precision in stillness is passing evermore

To choose that which we gnaw at ourselves with
our inner devil's eye
our unbecoming ally
acting, stand-in absolutes
when it is pouring, choose to be soaked
when in pain from mockery,
choose that misery
if embraced, choose that
which you are feeling
agency in destiny
that scab one is scratching
rather the boatman or the river
neither the boatman nor the river
we remain not to ask but to frame
that abandoned purgatorial afterword
agency reframes the story

An aspen branch
a smile at a loss
were that it was so
in dirty golden autumn
an aspen tree in a row
stood with its ilk, and I so solemn
followed a branch which hung askew
by a mere trinket of wood it hung from the trunk
and creaked in the wind

What was the creaking?
Was it Boreas' warning,
that in his domain in lieu
of play some will suffer and decay;
winter's grasp would snap the sinew
of the lone and daring branch?

Was it Zephyrus' plaything,
as he whistled and teased
of the hope of spring;
that which hadn't persevered
would by ants be used anew?

a close encounter
pale ivory bark with black wrinkles and buds
where glossy green leaves had grown to gold
What of the branch?
it is gone, so is the very tree
Earth shifted and parted as a sea,
and the tree floated, *that* we could not see,
into the rafters above our knowing
a space beyond falling
a smile at a loss
Were that it was so?

Artificial redemption

a robin, a jay, a magpie, and a blackbird
heard and flew to answer a call
on a bench in a park near a river there sat a dying bird
cracking, flaking, pealing was the paint of the bench
"Silver fiend, with aching grip have I been torn:
an artificer's small dreams;
my crafted fate's distant relations;
indignant claims unbound.
I have known the impediment of my call.
Where is the potence in the appeal of the sound
of laboured delineation with poetic license
of the turbulent winds that hurt me,
of the yellow-eyed predators that haunted me?
I refuse.
My silver fiend is a memory
of an admired appearing to me,
accusing me of insensitivity,
vanishing without a kiss after our dance.
Through the swooshing of playing leaves
atop swaying trees, the uncertainty
of its falsehood has wondered of me,
and I am become fleeting morning dew.
But my strange siblings of a strange minority:
I do not know of a better view.
You have witnessed my plea.
And in your presence, I find redemption anew,
For you have seen, you have heard, my call,
In your eyes, I find solace, a view so true,
In your presence, I am wealthy, standing tall."

Leafling

curtain call of the magician's first act at career's end
warm falling of daydreaming
a pine tree's leafling fails to hold on
drifting spiral wafting
rocked by a black and white magpie swarm
their coats of absolutes do not glisten
with light against the grey heaven
gliding past the pinecones their missions known
the Sun and it remain to be seen
and where if anywhere it will end
gliding downwind sprawling landscape of interjections
the teeth of a giant fallen
laden with earth and trees the nerves of its brain reaching uncontained
as the leafling glides downwind passing through an abandoned web
at the edge of a brook where it dances a pirouette
on the surface of the passing waters
sending a ripple whispering across the commute
of the water reaching the flowerless leaf of a water lily,
the anchor of the web,
across which a tremor shook
and it fell weaving with the wind a new shape
holding on to the pirouetting leafling
as a gale rose up and gave itself to them

Lit bonfire under the edge

lit bonfire under the edge
in the bowels of a decorative ridge of hills
of unreaped fields of rough, senescent gold
of a marched road of prescriptive droning drones
laid siege by the will of the flame; its great shape slopes
on the meandering tree line of the hills' forest
gesturing hands take note
nothing to hold its ardour

This makes us equal

When you turn around everything you know
Will be gone, yes it will all be gone
When you turn around, and you will
Everything you know will be gone
It will be gone

As you turn, the world will transform
The familiar sights and sounds, they conform
To a new reality, a different plane
Where what once was, will never be the same
Gone are the days of comfort and ease
As you navigate through uncharted seas
The people you love, the places you know
They fade away, like a distant echo
The dreams you once held close to your heart
Now seem distant, torn apart
As you turn, you must let go
Of the attachments that once made you whole
But fear not, for in this great shift
Lies the opportunity for a powerful lift
To discover new passions, new desires
To ignite the flames of your inner fires
For when you turn, you open the door
To endless possibilities, forevermore
You break free from the chains that bind
Let go of what you hold dear
And embrace the unknown with an open mind

A new weaving

Ye older sinners are not all the same.
The stitching does not hold together.
Seams are pulled apart as it is stretched
across the perceived slight on the memories
of your parents. Their ideals are not your tomorrow.
But that is all good and well
in the half-finished scarf of human history.
Yet strings do fly asunder and render
firm, woven images of acutely re-enacted
symbols of orders as pernicious
in their cyclical nature as the seasons
into stunned silences like that!
of a confused audience unsure
of what has transpired when an older sinner
turns around in their folding chair
and meeting the eyes of the onlookers
admits to cowardice and is humble
to the one young sinner, with whom
they broke bread and worked together...
Such is the beginning of a new weaving...

Restless beating

the unevenly betrayed mask
of dark tilled earth's longing
for the insipid, deeply sinking incisions
which, as the thunder tolled,
and the quickly spilling ink
of laboured confidence foretold
would wear down its resistor
who plough in hand would by lightning be met
across the restless beating of that
most insolvent estate

Embers

Whatever I was before
It doesn't matter anymore
Unbeknownst to the gates
Approaching evermore.
Through the unknown,
I make my way,
To a destination yet unseen,
What secrets lie beyond the fray,
I shall follow, my heart keen.
Through the veil, what ashes lie,
Beyond the veil, unknown and grand,
To the clearing's bonfire, I shall fly,
Where the smoke's embers still withstand
With longing eyes, I peer within,
At the remnants of a fading fire,
A testament to where I've been,
Surviving embers both hot and cold.

The Soothsayer

the soothsayer performs the ritual
stirs a pot of obscene content
reads the bones of sacrifices
flushes it all down the drain
and speaks the incantation: "irrelevance!"
the urchin awaiting an outcome mishears
and aloud wonders: "relevant events?"

What Rises beyond
life as dedication to that which rises beyond
slight slights to the imperative of categorization
I dare not leave the forest I have entered
a herd of goats grazed upon the forest trail
and took me for their shepherd
yesterday I dared not turn away from a fox
running across a thawing lake's surface

All its own
the place over which I have no map
for each it is their own
and rare are the commonalities
that do not end in bloodshed
but there is a place
a crafted place
of soft white beige sheets
of a palette of blue and white master brushstrokes
for which many sons and daughters have bled
of kingdoms whose last witnesses
have joined the sheets as dust
scooped up in swirls
by the breeze and carried off
somewhere, someplace
all its own

Aghast
thoughts come up again
they encompass a figure deliberating over and on
a precipice
a vast abyss beneath
the precipice crumbles without the figure moving
but before the plunge not felt and yet undertaken

by the brain of the figure absent of the self
the rock shelf gives way to sand
and the abyss rises up into a sinkhole
another shift and there is water now
before the figure drowns not having
raced for its final breath
it is standing in an empty land
on solid ground
each of its cells plunging, sinking, drowning
with mouth aghast the figure falls upwards

Meaning

I am not a junkyard dog
sniffing for an elusive bone.
I am that meagre, starved, half-blind, half-deaf mutt
scraping my back bloody against the fence,
as I crawl underneath and sniff about
running to the horizon with my ears fallen.

The Title

the eyes, they drift away
past the overt signifier
drawn, drifting away
the implicit, adjacent signified

The Frame

An ideological fantasy frame that we all embrace,
Where we're the exception, a unique case,
To find ourselves, we must first believe,
That we're the exception, and then perceive,
The truth that lies beyond this fantasy frame,
And discover who we truly are, without any shame.

A lone sparrow
Atop a tree, dead by winter wind, a lone sparrow sits
The morning sun, a golden hue, begins to rise,
Casting shadows upon its lonely guise.
With every gust, the sparrow sways its head,
An observer watches, his brow furrowed deep,
Pondering the hubris of his kind
In *that* part of his mind
For the avian had been made alone
As dark fumes had taken the rest
The sparrow, once a flock, now stands alone,
Lost to the fumes, its brethren gone.
He pays no notice to its beautiful plumage
Or its melancholy call
Or even that it has found a way to live on,
Thus adding to the world
He has found something to curse
He finds solace in his own despair,
Cursing the world, burdened with his share
In his heart, a fear takes hold,
That his soul is tainted, tarnished and cold
Is he afraid of hearing that which he suspects to be true?
That he is less akin to the sparrows and more akin
To the fumes...

A system so just
Behold, a realm of grandeur, their utmost delight,
Where distinctions of status were kept out of sight.
An overt creed of equality, a life so fair,
Can you fathom, oh dormant creature, lying there?
A structure in place, to hinder and defy,
The hoarding of riches, wealth's endless supply.
Where debts were settled regularly,
A system so just, a sight to see.

The Road as it is
imagine walking down a road upon which you have not travelled
for some time
during which time you have begun to attribute
a different significance to that road
and as you are walking you see in front of you
an eerie resemblance to your past self
with clothing you used to wear
and then a few steps in front of you
there lays a pigeon
with a tiny pool of blood next to its head
a sight which you had never before
beheld on that road

A whimper went unheard
To reach the pinnacle of wit,
Is to watch without judgment or critique.
For true intelligence lies in the ability to see,
Without bias or preconceived belief.

a whimper went unheard
leading a blustering dictation
insensitively accusing of insensitivity

Uncertainty
In the realm of psychological rewards,
The one-marshmallow circuit gleams,
A hyper-normal stimulus,
Detached from evolutionary dreams.
It seeks swift, instant certainty, without the toil
Of understanding,
No need to delve deep, no need for mental expanding.

Ah, but the two-marshmallow circuit,
A different tale it tells,
For it craves delayed gratification,
Where self-application dwells.
If my map of understanding is flawed or incomplete,
I'll embrace uncertainty, let go of moral conceit.

For instant reward, the one-marshmallow, belonging is the prize,
But it's hijacked by politics and corporations in disguise.
They discourage reading, discovery, and creative thought,
Instead, they offer false identities, battles to be fought.
Align with them, against the other, and you'll belong,
No need for personal growth, no need to be strong.
Certainty is handed to you, without earning its worth,
A premature gift, devoid of true wisdom's birth.

A single seed

a single seed of difference sprouts
between promises of energy's life
it must be minded as the last and
quintessential hope
a seed of and by the Earth holding
Man and beasts whole, it grows
a critical eye perceiving from wholeness
to which individuality is an obscenity

Vae Victis

Alas for the defeated, their fate sealed tight,
At the mercy of conquerors, no glimmer of light.
No leniency to expect, no mercy to implore,
Their pleas unheard, their hopes shattered to the core.
In ancient times, a tale of Rome's despair,
When Gauls attacked, leaving the city bare.

Except for the hill, where hope still clung,
Brennus besieged, victory on his tongue.
The Romans, desperate, sought to reclaim,
Their beloved city, their pride, their name.
A thousand pounds of gold, the price to pay,
To ransom their home, to keep the Gauls at bay.
But treachery lurked, deceit in the air,
The Romans accused, the weights unfair.
Brennus, unmoved, with a sword in hand,
Cried out, "Vae victis!" across the land.
The scales unbalanced, the burden increased,
More gold demanded, their anguish released.
Oh, the *woe of the vanquished*, their hearts torn,
For in defeat, their fate was forever sworn.

Orpheus

Orpheus, the famed musician of old,
Whose lyre's sweet strains could make the gods behold,
Was struck with grief when his dear wife was slain,
By a satyr's attack, in fields of grain.
Eurydice, fair and lovely to see,
Fell prey to vipers, and could not break free,
Her husband found her, lifeless and still,
And played such melodies, the world stood still.
The gods and nymphs, moved by his mournful tune,
Suggested he journey to the underworld soon,
To plead with Hades and Persephone,
To let Eurydice return with him.
They agreed, but with one condition to meet,
That Orpheus must not look back, nor retreat,
Until they both reached the upper world,
Where Eurydice's fate would be unfurled.
Alas, in his eagerness, Orpheus turned,
And saw his love, whom he had yearned,

To hold and cherish, once again,
But his mistake caused her to vanish, in pain.
Is there ever such a thing as loss or gain?
A warning to all who seek to retrieve,
What was lost: seeking what they had believed.

What is loved?
idiosyncratic handling of the illusion of the self
what you love of the one you love

Tantalus
Once hailed at Zeus' table, Tantalus, like Ixion,
Was embraced by divine grace,
Yet he betrayed the gods, a thief in their sacred space.
Ambrosia and nectar, he dared to steal,
To share with his people, their secrets to reveal.
But his most heinous act, a sacrifice so grim,
He offered his own son, Pelops, limb by limb.
Boiled and served as a feast for the divine,
To test their wisdom, their omniscient design.
The gods, repulsed by the gruesome sight,
Refrained from partaking, except for Demeter's plight.
Lost in grief for her daughter, she unknowingly ate,
A morsel of Pelops' shoulder, sealing his fate.
Zeus commanded Clotho, the Fate so wise,
To bring the boy back, to breathe life in his eyes.
She gathered the pieces, in a cauldron they were placed,
With an ivory shoulder, by Demeter graced.
Pelops, reborn, grew into a youth so fair,
Poseidon took him to Olympus, to teach and to share.
But Zeus, consumed by anger, cast him away,
For Tantalus' sins, he would forever pay.
Now Tantalus stands, in torment and despair,

In a pool of water, with fruit trees so rare.
As he reaches for sustenance, the branches rise,
Denying him nourishment, mocking his cries.
And when he bends to drink, the water retreats,
Leaving him parched, with unquenchable feats.
Above him, a stone looms, a menacing weight,
Like Sisyphus' burden, sealing his fate.
Eternally deprived of resources, Tantalus must endure,
A punishment so cruel, the future left forever unsure.
A reminder of his transgressions, his treacherous ways,
A life of eternal hunger, a soul forever ablaze.

The eyes of one I never knew

The eyes of a stranger, unknown to me,
Filled with darkness, tainted by sin's decree,
For a mere coin, their sanity they'd trade,
Yet, they could foresee what lay ahead, unswayed.
But their vision, alas, was clouded and blind,
Only glimpsing the unjust fate that would unwind,
Did they yearn, like me, for hope's sweet embrace,
Dreaming that each day's torment would find solace.
In this endless journey, we both strive,
To find respite from the pain that's alive,
Yet, their eyes, so distant, see beyond the now,
While I long for dreams to soothe my weary brow.
Oh, the eyes of one I never knew,
A reflection of my own sorrow, 'tis true,
In search of a dream, we both endure,
Gazing ahead, hoping for a future pure.

A nightmare

Alas, a nightmare where my dreams have fled,
Washed away like stains, leaving me in dread,
My feet now skittish, unsure where to tread,
I think I'll abstain from hopes that have bled.
The colour of my hands, I cannot disguise
Of the dreams that once were, now left behind,
My skittish feet, they dance with silent cries
Who hides in an outhouse, from the world outside?
A place to escape, where dreams can reside.
But who minds when they're gone, I and my unknown
When my dreams have gone, forever disowned?

Dopamine

Oh, dopamine, thou art not just for reward,
But for the thrill of what may come to pass.
Anticipation oft doth strike the chord,
And oft surpasses what we thought would last
Our economic system, fuelled by ancient sunlight,
Converts it to dopamine, a fleeting delight.
We consume resources, non-renewable and rare,
In hopes of a future that surpasses compare.
From poetry's verse to pleasures of the flesh,
Our dopamine system must swiftly refresh.
For if it lingers, the thrill will fade away,
What once brought elation, now feels mundane.
We grow accustomed to unexpected delight,
And soon it becomes our new normal, slight.
Our hunger returns, unsatisfied once more,
Seeking new joys, as we did before.

Endless plight

In depths of thought, my mind overflows,
With awe, I embrace Earth's body vast,
Bound by a web, my senses transpose,
As recognition soars, my spirit's cast.
Swiftly I descend, like a darkened dart,
Shot from the bow of terror's cruel might,
Guided unerring to this beating heart,
I plummet through the void, in endless flight

Who bears thy very stance

How did thy brain construct, thou may ask?
Genes played a part, but 'tis the environment's task.
From thy fetal days, 'til this morn's repast,
Stimuli shape genes, both on and off they cast.
Some genes, forever awakened they shall be,
Whilst others, forever slumbering, thou see.
Non-Mendelian traits, a marvel to behold,
Inherited not through genes, but stories untold.
The world in which thou didst develop, dear friend,
Impacts thy body's profile, 'til the very end.
When thou art with child, traits shall be passed,
Not through genes, but through the hormones amassed.
Parenting style, influenced by this dance,
Shaping a child who bears thy very stance.
Generations may witness this grand design,
Yet little is set in stone, 'tis truth divine.
At every stage, interventions may undo,
The imprints of biology, old and new.

Damnatio memoriae

For remembrance's scorn,
A soul condemned, from records torn.
Through paths of negation's sway,
History's truth, they seek to betray.
Depictions shattered, names erased,
Documents stripped, rewritten in haste.
Yet, in this act of vandal's might,
Martyrs emerge, bathed in light.
For the dishonoured, forever known,
Their memory etched, never to disown.
Damnatio memoriae, a paradox to see,
Preserving their infamy, for all to decree.
Let it be known, in this solemn plea,
Those who destroy, agents of memory.
Their actions, a testament to the past,
Ensuring remembrance, forever to last.

A minor miracle

Amidst this world of strife and hate,
Two men conversing peacefully,
On a lonely road in winter's state.
While chaos reigns and minds are lost,
These two stand firm in reasoned thought,
Their words a balm amidst the cost
Of battles fought and battles wrought.
A minor miracle, some may say,
To witness such a scene unfold,
But let us hope and strive each day,
For more such miracles to behold

Faces stark

Where dreams exhale, safety signs retreat,
Through mire and muck, they trudge with weary feet,
Alive, yet expressionless, their faces stark,
Rumours of sunrise, elsewhere, leave their mark.

The End of what we have known

Wherever you pierce me, you pierce yourself
You and I; we are the world holding hands
My furthest limbs are your supply chains
How have we survived
Since the war to end wars?
We have held hands since the trenches,
Through globalising our mind into one,
Though we know not the colours of our eyes
Notwithstanding proxy wars, of course
We are greedy after all you and I
And that above all is our sickness
But had we not held hands;
Had we not been interdependent
We would not have been incentivised to avoid war
But now, standing here together,
Fragility has befallen our held hands;
So needy have we become; you and I
Driven by our want, not our conscience
We radically financialized, deregulated
And globalized to feed our wants and desires
And what can we show for it?
For 70-odd years have we survived
But at what cost, my dear?
We have grown from 2 to 8 billion
Resource consumption per capita has grown 100 times
Compared to before the industrial revolution
We can call it our growth equation,

The child we had together,
For whose sake we remain together
And who brings us together
But our child is eating the world

Our child is eating the world.
A hundred trillion dollars per day flash before its eyes:
With two hands attached to every bill
Hands that frack, mine, extract and pollute,
Hands that govern, hands that salute,
Hands that hold onto other hands,
Hands that spawn more hands exponentially,
Faster and faster as its interest wanes,
Without which our child will collapse,
And we simply cannot hold on without them
And under the weight of our troubles,
The world crumbles.

Every bill that flashes before its eyes
Serves merely as a representation of value,
A symbol of game theoretic optionality.
It possesses no inherent worth,
Yet it captivates the senses with its boundless potential
To acquire any desired value.
The velocity at which it flashes increases,
As the uncertainty of how the environment will evolve
Remains unknown.
The swiftness of the adaptive response becomes paramount,
Along with the optionality it offers,
Rather than any specific value that may diminish in significance.
Each bill functions as a token for quantifiable, extractable,
And exchangeable value,
Standing in stark contrast to the most cherished treasures of the Soul.
This bill fuels a decentralized incentive system
That motivates all eight billion of us to decipher ways to obtain it,

As everything we desire necessitates its possession.
It compels us to explore novel approaches
And optimize existing methods.
Those who excel in this system amass more power,
Influencing legislation,
Shaping cultural values through media,
And changing the system to their advantage.
Those who oppose the system also oppose those who thrive within it,
Prompting the powerful to suppress dissenters.
The global market, a superorganism,
Relies on the collective efforts of all individuals
While simultaneously governing them.
It must perish or the world will perish,
Unless an alternative were to emerge
Where diverse forms of value cannot be assessed
Using a singular currency.
A fungible, global unitary currency
With its own internal financial mechanisms,
Such as interest that generates embedded growth obligations,
Proves incompatible with our future.
The reality of interest necessitates the expansion of the monetary supply,
As the population and the system itself continue to grow.
However, with planetary boundaries reached,
Perpetual growth becomes untenable.
Nevertheless, the monetary system persists
In expecting exponential growth year after year.
Instead of following the economy, money now drives it.
This embedded growth obligation stands at odds
With our current life and possible future
And with what our Earth can handle.
Financial services need to change
To no longer have an embedded growth obligation.

Every drop of rainwater everywhere now contains:
Fluorinated surfactants; man-made chemicals
(carcinogens and neurotoxins)
And those, my dear, are forever chemicals.
Our child? Do not worry.
If nothing changes, we'll watch it grow fatter,
And one day it'll roll over us and crush us.

Feud and Mead

Part 1 of Feud and Mead

His knees scrape, scrape, scraping...
He drags the child in his heart, wickedly taunting,
"Cry for help, then!"
He shouts at the child afraid of men.
Whose protests, whimpers: echoes that a cave deepen.
"...Matters not, all you do is cry wolf!
They are not so solitary, so lone...
Look into this glass shard, see who's really so alone!",
as he jabs it against the boy.
His pale little frame cannot put up
even an inch of moat,
to defend against the mead taken shape of man, who will goat
the feud taken shape of boy.

"One day..."
The boy whispers, afraid to say:
"Mind your tongue, nay,
your whole body, glowing with a dark star's ray.
Your hands on me, a transgression...
Under your foot, I must pay to mind my thoughts, pay!
One day, I'll escape to far away, end your oppression.
I'll pay no mind to what's left of you, a scar.
I'll imagine you regressing back into the black tar:
effervescent, putrid tar with pits of aggression.
Into the cave of my name, you've leaked and dripped:
trickling in, fossilized netherworld wanderer.
In the cave of my name,
cold hands have a reality tightly gripped.
Did Khnum feel foreboding
when he spun his potter's wheel?
In the cave of my name, a blind mute spun a potter's wheel.

His eyes and tongue grew,
but your shape was too late to repeal.
Your creation was as a calf
pieced together with discarded, rotting veal.
The dumb potter grew sight in time to reel,
at the putrid tar spun into shape of man;
at the empty blackness of your eyes, that of a seal.
But it was too late for his foreboding:
you were whole, close enough to feel.
Etched into the walls of the cave, your first word to him, "Heel!"
From the cave of my name, you are my dark star rising and I your meal."
What began by only trickling in, to beal
had become mead taken shape of man:
full blown necrosis.
The feud taken shape of boy cried out, "Let go, ...

Part 2 of Feud and Mead

"...Cancerous growth!
A mistake allowed to fester, an error of apoptosis!"
"Crying wolf again? A pity, that you should be alone
with such apparent woe." the man taunted
The boy kicked and pulled away when the man began laughing,
who chased and jumped while mocking,
"If, if, if, I was your cancer, the best you could hope for,
would be to be granulomatous."
The boy ran, sparing no morsel of strength,
in that sharp wilderness, the deep night masking it's breadth.
With his pace he was temeritous
and with his silence, despite the man's continued mockery, despiteous.
Giving chase, the man shrilly shouted, "I've known you to be riotous,
but your chosen actions being so repetitious
while knowing the oh-so-obvious outcome,
betrays your character as completely fatuous."
Amidst their cat and mouse chase, the boy made his path tortuous,

surprising the foaming chaser, now struggling and himself despiteous.
Two galloping pairs of feet;
Two rough, naked pairs of soles;
Bound not by birth or death but by common meat;
Brimming, spilling over the edge: passionate souls.
The man, licking lips, thoughts on desires, covetous
of the boy's spirit and its fate, making him solicitous.
The boy, convinced his pursuer was flagitious,
and that if recaptured, his fate, was to be made asomatous.
Drawing near, falling loudly but in the deep night achromatous.
To one, a chance, but to the one on his rear a great fear.
Drawing near, a test of desperation and temerity.
Their soles and souls at the edge...
Drawing near, displays of ability, agility, even fortuity.
As Fortuna spun her wheel, was it all chance or was fate foreordained
that night at the edge?
The little boy jumped down a tall, precipitous cliff: the threat of spectre.
As he fell with the water,
from the cliff came shrill shrieks by the shouter,
that shrunk in volume the farther,
he fell but like shrapnel, had made their impact.

Part 3 of Feud and Mead

Fear ruled the boy still: the result of long, dismal accretion.
Before any consideration could be given to current tract
he waited for a revealing act, for the peaceful serenity to end
after waking in a riverbend; feeling warmth from the sun.
Where to run or whether to run at all: left him to recogitate.
But hearing crows eight, spurred him out of the water.
The shouter shrieked through their loud caws.
Judging their netherworld maws, the boy stood his ground
hiding the pound, pound, pound of his heart
till they dart away: turning over the hourglass.
His fate played centre mass; round which all spun.

A punter in bright, warm lands with naught but his acumen
following the river in rags, devoid of prospects, hoping to find no men.
Clad in fur, older yet firm as stone,
fishing for abalone next to a house with legs of hen
stood a woman as lone as the boy yet calm and still who turned when
the boy approached her and stared *deep* into his eyes till she had her fill.
"So young, yet your sand is running out,
darkness wants your heart to *keep*.
Give me your hand." she said and with a gentleness
gave him cooked abalone.
In judging her, he found her warmth did suppress his inner distress.
So, he sat with her, watching her make jewellery from the shells,
asking her, "Are you a fortune teller?
Or could you magically change my fortune?"
"I'm nor teller nor seer.
My power is from devilry, stronger in light of moon.
You need not fear. That is our similarity. Our pain,
that of a torrential monsoon.
I cannot your fate veer.
It is your responsibility. But I will help you weather it."
As she gave him to wear a shell necklace, they smiled merrily
in light of such a boon.
His fate he could bear, a little more each day, and less wearily,
in that house with legs of hen,
where he did hear and learn her melancholy melodies of psaltery;
where his worn rags she replaced with soft, sturdy furs,
seeing his scarred skin,
where he did all to earn her hard-earned lively giggle;
where he did adorn every room with his lively presence, in her eyes;
where she did yearn to impart use of parchment and abacus skilfully;
where thoughts forlorn were left at the door in that, a beloved and
benevolent home.
A day came with churning stomachs, sour tempers and
worded ire not meant,

just a day and yet anything but; when soar above did four crows,
maws with foam.
The sunny skies began to blacken;
more and more did he feel the weight of his fate.
Had Helios decided to abandon them or had a greater force
spun his wheels into upset?
Fearful and enamoured, "For none but you." she said,
and threw the boy down a hidden hatch
The shrill shouting tore down the door and the man heard
one with gravitas say, "Reprobate!
I have taken his fate away from your cold hands. My heart
is immutable as is my rectitude."
Hidden from prying eyes, the boy watched a blaze light up the night
and break his heart.

Part 4 of Feud and Mead

Travelling blindly, from river to thicket to forest with no sense of time,
only of plight.
Looking up only when the blackened skies waned
though it gave him no sense of ease.
All flying creatures did he curse,
and to the sands of time he gave no more thought.
Clutching the necklace, with remorse for worded ire not meant,
trapped in memory maze...
Falling from exhaustion, his fading force made abject through
abnegation of all but sunlight...
"Please...
...she lit a little light..."

Quickly fading whimpers of fear of death did his mind seize,
reminiscent of echoes that a cave deepen,
and did take hold of his last heartbeat.
Bare, lonely cries of a thing small and weak
spurred him up to his feet with its pleas.

Through thick bushes its call did he seek,
the thorns dug deep, red drops stole his sight.
He saw young hands of one tall and sleek
around the neck of a black raven.
He freed the fearful creature from a cruel fate,
and turned to face and fight
a maiden with aberrant feature: putrid, black tar gushed down her chin
who stood caught in fright and cowered,
having picked neither flight nor fight.
He reached out with gentle hand, she recoiled,
and he knew her fate when
he saw her well-worn rags and her figure, bonier than he had ever been
and when he to her hummed a melancholy melody,
she grew mad and mean.
"You need not fear. Your pain is mine, our similarity.
I have your past seen.
I am no mere seer. They reign, but slain you are not.
Give me your hand."
With a gentle tear, she took the shell necklace.
And with another his hand.
She would bear her fate, a little more each day, and the tar would end.
And her fear, and her hate, a little more each day, would dissipate.
And to care for her would his heart, a little more each day, satiate.
Till a single crow cawed for him and four ravens croaked for her.
Whose end and whose start had the fateful Wheel of Life spun to?

Part 5 of Feud and Mead

To mend her heart did reset his gaze, fill his will, raise his chin.
The crow sent to bait, sent to faze, did only fail its master of sin,
for their foe took the bait, feeling full of might, to end his plight.
The bellicose expatriate went back to the birth of his plight.
His morose thoughts did relent in light of odyssey of love filled might
of those whose hearts had burnt ever so brightly in his name
and of those whose lives he brought out of misery to a better time.

Climbing the rows of jagged cliff teeth;
Hearing the blows of thunder's master of sin seethe;
Feeling old woes reduced to droplets falling on that dark heath;
Waiting calm and still, firm as stone, for evil known.
With mocking tone, the man did groan and moan while
mocking the boy's climbing, but to the boy he did drone.
Sensing how apollonian his pawn, he grew mad and mean.
Dashing at the boy with glass shard, then stunned having seen
unflinching pawn evaded him with stoic ease.
Striking flash of bright lightning illuminated
shifting shadows.
Dropping his sharp shard in shock of dwindling might,
shrinking hands.
Pieces of cliff shot down under growing weight
with waning blackened skies...
The boy did grow fonder of attained new shape
with every step.
The man did cower as fear did cover his nape
with glistening sweat.
The boy did saunter with amenity of favourable fate.
The **M**aligned **E**ntity **A**trociously **D**amaging
shrunk down to shape of boy as,
the **F**avourable **E**ntity **U**nder **D**evelopment
took shape of man.

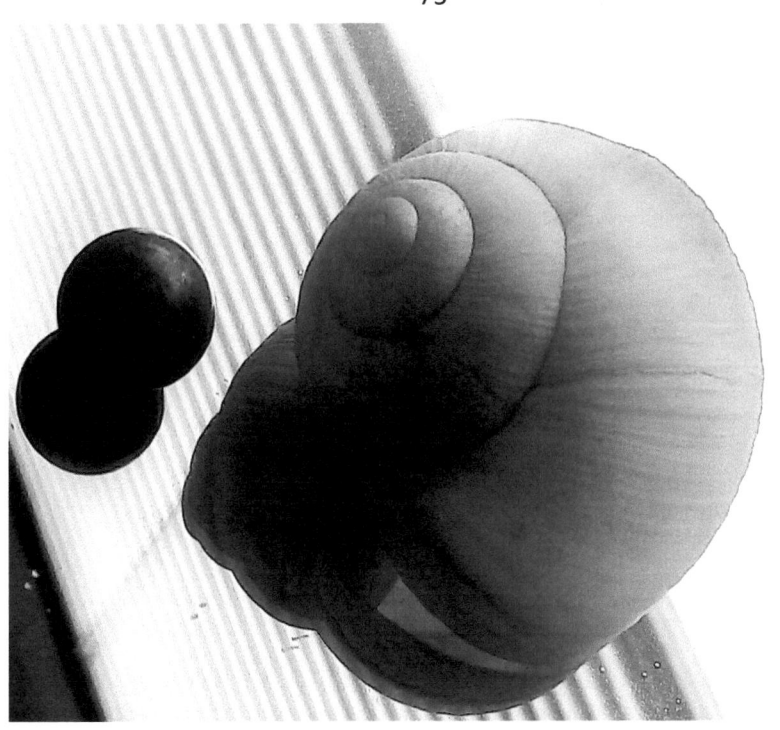

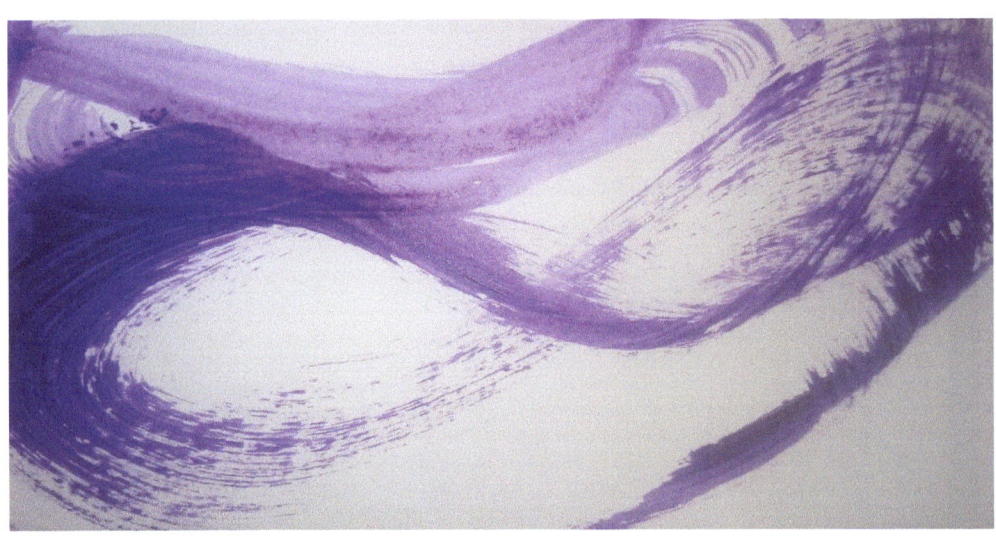

As you lift your gaze from this page
you will be as me, and together we will be
guests of rising glances.